First Edition

How To Keep More of What You Win

A Gambler's Guide to Taxes

By Walter L. Lewis, CPA

Impulse Publishing, Inc.

WARNING–DISCLAIMER

It should be clearly understood that neither the author nor the publisher of this book are engaged in any way in providing legal, accounting, tax, or other professional services. This book has been published in order to provide our readers with accurate, authoritative information, that they can then use to supplement, compliment, and amplify other existing information that is available about Gaming and Taxes. We advise you to read and study as many of these materials as you can and urge you to consult with a legal, accounting, or tax professional in regard to any questions you may have about your own taxes or gambling winnings and losses.

This book is to be used as a general guide and source of background information about gambling and taxes. We hope that it will help you to plan wisely and to avoid some common tax liability pitfalls. We do not, however, suggest, imply, or recommend in any way, that readers can use this book to avoid paying taxes that they legally owe. The information contained here is meant to help you become more familiar with the laws as they are and how to obey and use them wisely. It should also be understood that text may contain errors, typographical or otherwise, and the information given will be outdated, if tax laws or regulations change after the printing date.

The publishers and author recognize revenue procedures and tax forms are in the public domain. However, their arrangement and compilation along with the other material in this guide are subject to the copyright notice. The purpose of the book is to entertain and educate our readers. The author and publishers shall have neither responsibility or liability to any person or entity with respect to any loss or damage caused, or alleged to be caused, directly or indirectly by the information contained in this book.

If you do not wish to be bound by the above, you may return this book with proof of purchase within thirty days to the publisher for a full refund.

Your questions, comments, and suggestions are welcomed by the author, and can be mailed to him at this address:

Walter L. Lewis, CPA, 1776 Warren Road, Indiana, Pa. 15701

For distribution and marketing information, write or call:

Impulse Publishing, Inc.
c/o Kelly Simon Productions
1600 Ranch Drive
Latrobe, PA 15650
1-800-747-5599

- Editing by Kelly Simon and Geoff Miller
- Design by Angela Merendino
- Photographs of Mr. Lewis by Charles Sartoris
- Cover photography by Masterfile Images: Pierre Arsenault, Greg Stott, Alec Pytlowany, and Paul Terpanjian

Printed in the United States of America.
Library of Congress Catalog Card Number 96-95259
ISBN # 0-9655716-0-2

Industry Leaders Praise
HOW TO KEEP MORE OF WHAT YOU WIN

"This is a must-have resource for beginners and experienced players alike. Answers key questions and provides clear answers and recommendations and should make your taxman happy, for you'll have kept proper documentation for him and the IRS, thus removing potential stress for everyone when it comes to proving gambling wins and losses. A fine time-saver too (tells you what forms you'll need under what circumstances), and for the price, author Lewis does a bang-up job of helping anyone avoid costly mistakes."

– Howard Schwartz, Marketing Director
Gamblers Book Shop, Las Vegas, Nevada

"Walter Lewis takes the gamble out of tax matters for consistent winners or even the lucky player who strikes it rich. Entertaining, a joy to read, with a helpful step-by-step approach."

– Review excerpt by Eddie Olsen,
Editor & Publisher
Blackjack Confidential Magazine

HERE ARE JUST SOME OF THE FEATURES OF THIS VALUABLE GUIDE:

- Specific ways to reduce the time you spend and the fees you pay to your tax preparer
- How to determine what is and is not an allowable gaming deduction
- Valuable insights into how the IRS views gaming activity
- How to document your gaming activities and how to report it to the IRS
- How to avoid the costly mistakes that can raise your tax bill with the IRS
- Answers to fifteen of the most frequently asked questions about gambling and taxes
- A comprehensive index designed to let you swiftly find the solution to your special needs

All of the above are just part of the total approach that makes
HOW TO KEEP MORE OF WHAT YOU WIN
the best book on gambling and taxes available today!

ACKNOWLEDGMENTS

A very special note of thanks to Kelly Simon for her support, enthusiasm and belief in this project.

Thanks to my wife, Suzanne, for being my initial sounding board and helping with the original text.

Finally, thanks to a special group of individuals whose adventures convinced me of the need for this book.

PREFACE

This Guide is designed to provide accurate and authoritative information in regard to the subject matter covered. It is sold with the understanding that neither the author nor the publisher are engaged in rendering legal, accounting, tax or other professional services. If legal, accounting, tax or other expert assistance is required, the services of a competent professional person should be sought.

The author invites you to send questions you would like to see addressed in future editions. Address your questions to:

Walter L. Lewis, CPA
1776 Warren Road
Indiana, PA 15701

The publishers and author recognize revenue procedures and tax forms are in the public domain. However, their arrangement and compilation along with the other material in this guide are subject to the copyright notice.

ABOUT THE AUTHOR
Walter L. Lewis, CPA

Walt is one of the founding partners of Smith, Lewis, Chess & Company, a CPA firm with three offices in Southwestern Pennsylvania. He is a current member of both the Pennsylvania and the American Institute of Certified Public Accountants. He earned a B.S. in Business Management with a concentration in accounting from Indiana University of Pennsylvania, (IUP). His twenty-five years experience, along with his respected financial opinions have earned him positions on the advisory boards of numerous institutions and privately held corporations. He takes great pride in being able to present complicated tax issues in an understandable way.

Dedicated to the memory of
Walter and Laura Lewis,
who encouraged me to take a chance,
roll the dice and always make the best
out of the hand life dealt me.

TABLE OF CONTENTS

Figure A
Casino Game Played Most Often
(among those who gambled)

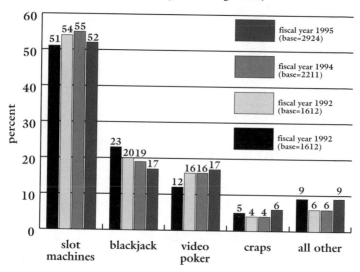

	fiscal year 1995 (base=2924)
	fiscal year 1994 (base=2211)
	fiscal year 1992 (base=1612)
	fiscal year 1992 (base=1612)

The proportion of gamblers who said they play slot machines most often, after rising from 1992 to 1994, fell back down to 1992 levels, to 52% currently. Players of video poker continued to increase slightly this year: the 1995 figure stood at 17%, compared to 12% in 1992. The proportion of gamblers who said they play blackjack most often continued to go down, to 17% currently, from 23% in 1992 (Figure A).

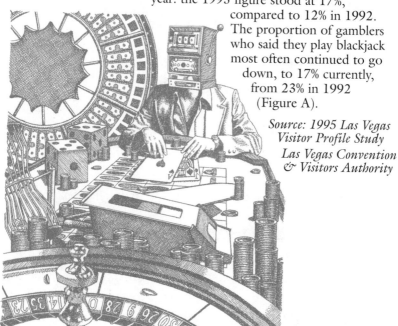

Source: 1995 Las Vegas Visitor Profile Study
Las Vegas Convention & Visitors Authority

Chapter One

INTRODUCTION

To gamble legally in the United States between 1910 and 1930, one had to go to race tracks in Maryland or Kentucky. During the Depression, Nevada relegalized gambling and other states allowed wagering at race tracks. In 1964 New Hampshire held the first state lottery. Today, more people are gambling than ever before, and both the number of gamblers and the amount of their wagers are expected to grow. All but two states now have some form of legalized gambling, and it is appearing in many new environments; on Indian reservations, riverboats, the Internet and on international air flights.

The Internal Revenue Service (IRS) is well aware of this increase in activity. For the IRS this increase is a win-win situation. More players mean there will be more taxable winnings. Since losses can be deducted only to the extent of the winnings, the IRS has no fear of having to give back any tax dollars to losers. By enforcing strict regulations to substantiate losses and creating additional tax liability even after deducting those losses, the IRS looks at gamblers as a large potential source of new tax revenue.

This guide contains answers to fifteen of the most frequently asked questions about the tax treatment of gambling winnings and losses. Also included is a reproduction of Revenue Procedure 77-29 which provides guidelines to gamblers for tax purposes. Samples of tax forms as well as information about completing them are included.

Gambling winnings and losses can significantly impact your tax liability and your obligation to properly report income. Information contained in this document is, in most cases, very general. After reading it, you may wish to discuss your personal situation with your tax consultant.

A taxpayer is permitted to deduct gambling losses against the value of complimentary goods and services provided by the casino (comps).

Robert Libutti v. Commissioner

Don't be a "Louie the Loser"

Wally the Winner and Louie the Loser are the best of friends. They do many things together, but their recreation-of-choice is gambling.

Casinos and the tracks are their favorites, and although they go there together, their style of play is almost totally different.

At the track, Wally studies the program and handicaps the horses before making his wager. Louie sits at the bar until a minute before post time, then runs to the window and bets on a hunch.

When the evening is over, Wally saves his tickets and records his winnings and losses in his gambling journal. Louie rips up his losers, cusses, blames the jockeys, and swears he'll never come back, (until the next time, anyway).

On trips to the casinos, Wally sticks to a system and plays within controlled limits. As always, he finishes his session by documenting the evening's activities.

Louie, on the other hand, sits at the blackjack table and bets erratically. Sometimes hitting sixteen when the dealer shows a face card, sometimes not. Sometimes hitting thirteen when the dealer shows a six, sometimes not. On rare occasions, he actually wins, and proclaims himself "The Greatest Blackjack Player of All Time". Louie finally leaves before the other players have him removed from the table. He decides to join the fun at the craps table.

There, he jumps between the pass and don't pass line, makes mostly wrong choices, and blames the shooter. Within a short period of time, Louie leaves, much to the relief of the other players.

At the end of the day, Wally meets Louie at the buffet. Wally listens to Louie's tales of woe, hears about how close Louie came to breaking even and how he knows his luck is going to change. Louie also tells Wally about all the new friends he met while playing. Wally usually picks up the check, since Louie is almost always broke.

At the end of the year, Wally tallies his winnings at $10,000 with documented losses of $8,000.

Louie has no clue how much he lost during the year, but guesses it to be around $18,000. Since he hasn't kept a journal, there is no way for him to know for sure.

For Louie, when it comes to gambling and taxes, Murphy's Law prevails. On New Year's Eve, Wally has a date. Louie must make their annual trip to the casinos to bet and to watch the bowl games himself.

4

As Louie enters his first casino, he decides to do something different - kill some time at the slot machines. He searches for a machine that he knows is "ready to hit", throws in three silver dollars and something astounding happens!! He hits...BIG TIME!! Bells ring, sirens scream and lights flash.

Casino officials rush over to congratulate him and arrange his payout...$20,000. Louie won $20,000!

The first thing they do is ask him to sign form W-2G, which they are required by law to send to the Internal Revenue Service. Already shocked, Louie is now in a panic. He begs and pleads with them not to tell the IRS about his win, but there is nothing they can do. It's the law.

Louie now thinks of his buddy Wally and all the time he has spent documenting his gambling activity – winnings and losses – and wonders where his first big win will leave him with the IRS.

He will now be on record with the IRS as a $20,000 winner. The only loss he could document is the $3.00 he played to win the $20,000.

Had he kept a journal, Louie could have deducted his $18,000 in losses. But you guessed it, the IRS now considers him to be a $19,997.00 winner and will tax him accordingly.

Louie is a loser. Wally is a winner because **WALLY READ THIS BOOK.**

The moral of the story: ***Don't gamble unless you are prepared to win.***

LVCVA

The Las Vegas Convention & Visitors Authority's Most Asked Research Questions

Question About Las Vegas	Answer 1994	1995
1. How many visitors come to Las Vegas?	28,214,362	29,002,122
2. What is the projected 1996 visitor volume?		30.3 Million
3. What is tourism's economic impact?	$19.2 Billion	$20.7 Billion
4. How many convention delegates visit?	2,684,171	2,924,879
5. How many conventions were held?	2,662	2,826
6. What is Clark County's gaming revenue?	$5.4 Billion	$5.7 Billion
7. What is Las Vegas' gaming revenue?	$4.4 Billion	$4.5 Billion
8. What is the average gambling budget per trip?	$480	$514
9. What is the city-wide occupancy?	89.0%	88.0%
10. What is the Las Vegas hotel occupancy?	92.6%	91.4%
11. What is the Las Vegas motel occupancy?	73.2%	72.4%
12. What is the Las Vegas weekend occupancy?	94.4%	93.5%
13. What is the US national average occupancy?	64.7%	65.5%
14. Total enplaned/deplaned airline passengers?	26,850,486	28,027,239
15. Scheduled enplaned/deplaned passengers?	21,577,193	23,247,015
16. Charter enplaned/deplaned passengers?	4,068,106	3,799,290
17. Average daily traffic-all major highways?	56,875	58,917
18. How many new rooms were added in Las Vegas?	2,816	2,999
19. What is the average nightly room rate?	$52	$54
20. How many Las Vegas hotel/motel rooms?	88,560	90,046
21. What is the average # of nights stayed?	3.1 nights	3.5 nights
22. What percent of visitors are under 21?	8%	11%
23. What percent of visitors arrive by air?	44%	44%
24. What percent of visitors arrive by auto?	39%	41%
25. What percent of visitors are from So. Calif.?	30%	32%
26. What percent of visitors are international?	14%	13%

Source: Las Vegas Convention and Visitors Authority
Marketing Research Department
(702) 892-0711

updated 2/27/96

Chapter
Three

QUESTIONS AND ANSWERS

---

1. **What types of activities are included in reportable gambling winnings?**

   Reportable gambling winnings include, but are not limited to, lotteries, bingo, raffles, horse and dog racing, and all casino activities.

2. **Am I responsible to report only the winnings that have been reported to me by the gambling establishment?**

   No. You must report all winnings. The diary you keep (see question 13) must document all winnings and losses.

3. **By "all winnings" do you mean all winnings from legal activities?**

   No. All winnings include winnings from both legal and illegal activities.

4. How do I report my gambling winnings?

Gambling winnings are reported on Form 1040 of the U.S. Individual Income Tax Return on the "Other Income line".

5. Can I write off my gambling losses?

You may write off your gambling losses to the extent of your gambling winnings on Schedule A -Itemized Deductions as an "Other Miscellaneous Deduction".

6. I itemize deductions and I am able to substantiate more losses than winnings. May I deduct the excess losses?

No. Losses are deductible only to the extent of gambling winnings.

7. I file a joint return with my spouse. I had substantial documented losses in 1995, while my spouse had gambling winnings. May we combine our winnings and losses on our 1995 tax return?

Yes. If a husband and wife file a joint return, they may combine losses and deduct to the extent of both spouses winnings.

8. **In 1995, I won money playing blackjack, lost money playing the state lottery, and lost money betting on the horses. Do I have to report each activity separately?**

   No. Losses from one type of gambling activity may be offset against gains from another type of gambling activity.

9. **In 1994, I had gambling losses that exceeded gambling winnings by a substantial amount. In 1995 my gambling winnings exceeded my gambling losses. May I use the unused portion of my 1994 losses to offset my 1995 winnings?**

   No. Gambling losses can only be used to offset gambling winnings during the same year. Excess gambling losses may not be carried forward or carried back to any other tax year.

10. **If I have gambling losses equal to or greater than my gambling winnings, there will be no effect on my tax liability because one will offset the other. Is this right?**

    Not necessarily.

    First, you need to have proper substantiation for the losses you are claiming (see question number 13). Without appropriate documentation losses could be disallowed by the IRS.

    Next, you must itemize deductions in order to claim your losses. You will only itemize your deductions if they exceed the standard deduction amount. For 1996 the standard deduction amount for a single taxpayer is

$4,000. For a married couple filing a joint return the amount is $6,700.

Finally, by including winnings in gross income on Form 1040, your adjusted gross income will be increased. The adjusted gross income amount could impact many calculations you may be subject to. As an example:

- If you receive social security benefits, a larger dollar amount may be taxable.

- If you itemize deductions and have deductible medical expenses, a smaller dollar amount will be deductible.

- If you itemize deductions and have deductible job related and other miscellaneous expenses, a smaller dollar amount will be deductible.

11. I know my gambling losses far exceed my gambling winnings. If I include my winnings in gross income, and losses as an itemized deduction to the extent of the winnings, will I be challenged by the IRS?

You could be. Just as you could be challenged by the IRS for any of the items on your return. However, if you have reported all of your winnings and have the proper documentation to support your losses, you will feel more comfortable answering any questions the IRS may ask you.

12. Will the IRS accept my gambling losses if they do not exceed my gambling winnings?

Your gambling losses must be substantiated with adequate documentary evidence if you are challenged by the IRS.

13. Will the IRS accept my statement that my gambling losses exceed my gambling winnings?

No. There are guidelines recommended in Revenue Procedure 77-29, that should be followed to substantiate losses. (See Chapter IV)

14. What is Revenue Procedure 77-29?

Revenue Procedure 77-29 provides taxpayers with guidelines concerning the treatment of both gambling winnings and losses and the responsibility for maintaining adequate documentation of winnings and losses. This Procedure is reprinted in Chapter IV.

15. I did not report my gambling winnings and losses in 1994. What should I do?

You have three years to file Form 1040X and amend the information contained in your original return. If you filed your 1994 tax return by April 15, 1995, you have until April 15, 1998 to file an amendment. (See example in Chapter VII)

Losing Tickets

Losing tickets are popular means of substantiating losses. Tickets that are numbered sequentially, clean and untorn will help you in substantiating losses.

Taormina v. Commissioner

In contrast, the court threw out tickets that were covered with heel marks.

Green v. Commissioner

Likewise, tickets that were out of sequence will not help substantiate claimed losses.

Saitta v. Commissioner

©SCW, INC.

Chapter Four

SUBSTANTIATING LOSSES

The Internal Revenue Service issues Revenue Procedures on various subjects that effect the rights and duties of the taxpayers under the Internal Revenue Code. These procedures are considered to be matters of public knowledge. If gambling winnings and losses are claimed, the IRS will require compliance with Revenue Procedure 77-29.

What the IRS expects you to know:

Revenue Procedure 77-29 provides guidelines concerning the proper treatment of wagering gains and losses for federal income tax purposes. More importantly, it discusses the taxpayers' responsibility for maintaining adequate records to support the claimed gains and losses. By providing these guidelines to the taxpayer, it also provides the IRS agent with guidelines to support the agent's claim that deductions should not be allowed.

Your gambling diary:

The IRS has not issued a preprinted format where the taxpayer can fill in the blanks and be certain the information will, without questions, be accepted. Therefore, knowledge of the information contained in Revenue Procedure 77-29 becomes extremely important. The Revenue Procedure requires the taxpayer to maintain, on a regular basis, an accurate diary, log, or similar record that is supported by appropriate evidence of both winnings and losses. Records should include:

- The type of gambling activity.

- The date the activity took place.

- Where the activity took place.

- Who the taxpayer was with.

- A statement of amount won and/or lost.

Additional documented evidence of gambling winnings and losses could include appropriately dated:

- Airline or bus ticket to the gambling location

- Hotel charges

- Cash credit card advances

- Bank withdrawals

- Casino statement

- Race track program

- Unredeemed race track tickets

- Unredeemed lottery tickets

More specific guidelines for various gambling activities are presented in the Revenue Procedure that follows.

REVENUE PROCEDURE 77-29

Section 1. Purpose

The purpose of this revenue procedure is to provide guidelines to taxpayers concerning the treatment of wagering gains and losses for federal tax purposes and the related responsibility for maintaining adequate records in support of winnings and losses.

Section 2. Background

Income derived from wagering transactions is includible in gross income under the provisions of section 61 of the Internal Revenue Code of 1954. Losses from wagering transactions are allowable only to the extent of gains from such transactions, under section 165(d) of the Code, and may be claimed only as an itemized deduction.

Temporary regulations section 7.6041-1 (T.D. 7492, 1977-2 C.B. 463), effective May 1, 1977, require all persons in a trade or business who, in the course of that trade or business, make any payment of $1,200 or more in winnings from a bingo game or slot machine play, or $1,500 or more in winnings from a keno game, to prepare Form W-2G, Statement for Certain Gambling Winnings, for each person to whom the winnings are paid.

In determining whether such winnings equal or exceed the $1,500 reporting floor and in determining the amount to be reported on Form W-2G in the case of a keno game, the amount of winnings from any one game shall be reduced by the amount wagered for that one game. In the case of bingo or slot machines, the total winnings will not be reduced by the amount wagered. Forms W-2G reporting such payments must be filed with the Internal Revenue Service on or before February 28 following the year of payment.

Winnings of $600 or more, unreduced by the amount of the wagers, must also be reported for every person paid gambling winnings from horse racing, or jai alai, if such winnings are at least 300 times the amount wagered.

Winnings of $600 or more, unreduced by the amount of the wagers, must also be reported for every person paid gambling winnings from state conducted lotteries.

Under Section 6001 of the Code, taxpayers must keep records necessary to verify items reported on their income tax returns. Records supporting items on a tax return should be retained until statute of limitations on that return expires.

Section 3. Procedures

An accurate diary or similar record regularly maintained by the taxpayer, supplemented by verifiable documentation will usually be acceptable evidence for substantiation of wagering winnings and losses. In general, the diary should contain at least the following information:

1. Date and type of specific wager or wagering activity;

2. Name of gambling establishment;

3. Address or location of gambling establishment;

4. Name(s) of other person(s) (if any) present with taxpayer at gambling establishment; and

5. Amount(s) won or lost.

Verifiable documentation for gambling transactions include but is not limited to Forms W-2G; Forms 5754, Statement by Person Receiving Gambling Winnings; wagering tickets, cancelled checks, credit records, bank withdrawals, and statements of actual winnings or payment slips provided to the taxpayer by the gambling establishment.

Where possible, the diary and available documentation generated with the placement and settlement of a wager should be further supported by other documentation of the taxpayer's wagering activity or visit to a gambling establishment. Such documentation includes, but is not limited to, hotel bills, airline tickets, gasoline credit cards, cancelled checks, credit records, bank deposits, and bank withdrawals.

Additional supporting evidence could also include affidavits or testimony from responsible gambling officials regarding wagering activity.

The Service is required to report to the Congress by 1979 on the issue of whether casino winnings should be subject to withholding. In the absence of legislation requiring withholding on casino winnings, the instructions for preparing Form 5754 will not be applicable to winnings from keno, bingo, or slot machines. However, all other items of documentation to verify gambling losses from casino winnings are applicable.

With regard to specific wagering transactions, winnings and losses may be further supported by the following items:

.01   **Keno** – Copies of keno tickets purchased by the taxpayer and validated by the gambling establishment, copies of the taxpayer's casino credit records, and copies of the taxpayer's casino check cashing records.

.02   **Slot Machines** – A record of all winnings by date and time that the machine was played. (In Nevada, the machine number is the number required by the State Gaming Commission and may or may not be displayed in a prominent place on the machine. If not displayed on the machine, the number may be requested from the casino operator.)

.03   **Table Games: Twenty one (Blackjack), Craps, Poker, Baccarat, Roulette, Wheel of Fortune, Etc.** – The number of the table at which the taxpayer was playing. Casino credit card data indicating whether the credit was issued in the pit or at the cashier's cage.

.04   **Bingo** – A record of the number of games played, cost of tickets purchased and amounts collected on winning tickets. Supplemental records include any receipts from the casino, parlor, etc.

.05   **Racing: Horse, Harness, Dog, Etc.** – A record of the races, entries, amounts of wagers, and amounts collected on winning tickets and amounts lost on losing tickets. Supplemental records include unredeemed tickets and payment records from the racetrack.

.06 Lotteries – A record of ticket purchases, dates, winnings and losses. Supplemental records include unredeemed tickets, payment slips and winnings statements.

The recordkeeping suggestions set forth above are intended as general guidelines to assist taxpayers in establishing their reportable gambling gains and deductible gambling losses. While following these will enable most taxpayers to meet their obligations under the Internal Revenue Code, these guidelines cannot be all inclusive and the tax liability of each depends on the facts and circumstances of particular situations.

Losses can only be claimed as itemized deductions unless the taxpayer is in the trade or business of gambling.

Revenue Rulings 54-339 and 83-130

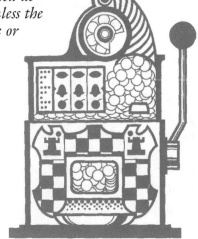

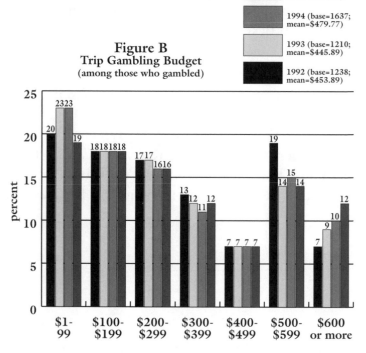

Figure B
Trip Gambling Budget
(among those who gambled)

1995 (base=2346; mean=$513.73)

1994 (base=1637; mean=$479.77)

1993 (base=1210; mean=$445.89)

1992 (base=1238; mean=$453.89)

The average gambling budget has increased significantly from $453.89, $445.32, $479.77, and $513.73 in 1992, 1993, 1994, and 1995 respectively (Figure B).

Source: *1995 Las Vegas Visitor Profile Study*
          Las Vegas Convention & Visitors Authority

Entries to your diary or log must be made when the gambling activity takes place. Your records may be determined to be inadequate if a hand writing expert testifies many of the entries were made at the same time.

Showell v. Commissioner

Chapter Five

REPORTING YOUR GAMBLING
WINNINGS AND GAMBLING LOSSES

Gambling winnings are reported on the line for "other income" on Form 1040. Since other items are also reported on this line, you must insert the word Gambling in the space provided. See the next page.

Gambling Winnings

Form **1040**	Department of the Treasury—Internal Revenue Service **U.S. Individual Income Tax Return** 1996	(99)	IRS Use Only—Do not write or staple in this space.

For the year Jan. 1–Dec. 31, 1996, or other tax year beginning , 1996, ending , 19 | OMB No. 1545-0074

Label (See page 11.) **Use the IRS label.** Otherwise, please print or type.	L A B E L H E R E	Your first name and initial	Last name		Your social security number
		If a joint return, spouse's first name and initial	Last name		Spouse's social security number
		Home address (number and street). If you have a P.O. box, see page 11.		Apt. no.	For help finding line instructions, see pages 2 and 3 in the booklet.
		City, town or post office, state, and ZIP code. If you have a foreign address, see page 11.			

Presidential Election Campaign (See page 11.) ► Do you want $3 to go to this fund? . . . . | Yes | No | Note: Checking "Yes" will not change your tax or reduce your refund.
If a joint return, does your spouse want $3 to go to this fund? . . . .

Filing Status

Check only one box.

1 ☐ Single
2 ☐ Married filing joint return (even if only one had income)
3 ☐ Married filing separate return. Enter spouse's social security no. above and full name here. ► _____
4 ☐ Head of household (with qualifying person). (See instructions.) If the qualifying person is a child but not your dependent, enter this child's name here. ► _____
5 ☐ Qualifying widow(er) with dependent child (year spouse died ► 19). (See instructions.)

Exemptions

If more than six dependents, see the instructions for line 6c.

6a ☐ Yourself. If your parent (or someone else) can claim you as a dependent on his or her tax return, **do not** check box 6a . . . .
b ☐ Spouse . . . .
c Dependents:

(1) First name Last name	(2) Dependent's social security number. If born in Dec. 1996, see inst.	(3) Dependent's relationship to you	(4) No. of months lived in your home in 1996

No. of boxes checked on lines 6a and 6b ____
No. of your children on line 6c who:
• lived with you ____
• did not live with you due to divorce or separation (see instructions) ____
Dependents on 6c not entered above ____
Add numbers entered on lines above ► ☐

d Total number of exemptions claimed . . . .

Income

Attach Copy B of your Forms W-2, W-2G, and 1099-R here.

If you did not get a W-2, see the instructions for line 7.

Enclose, but do not attach, any payment. Also, please enclose Form 1040-V (see the instructions for line 62).

7	Wages, salaries, tips, etc. Attach Form(s) W-2	7	
8a	**Taxable** interest. Attach Schedule B if over $400	8a	
b	Tax-exempt interest. DO NOT include on line 8a . . ☐ 8b		
9	Dividend income. Attach Schedule B if over $400	9	
10	Taxable refunds, credits, or offsets of state and local income taxes (see instructions) .	10	
11	Alimony received	11	
12	Business income or (loss). Attach Schedule C or C-EZ	12	
13	Capital gain or (loss). If required, attach Schedule D	13	
14	Other gains or (losses). Attach Form 4797	14	
15a	Total IRA distributions . . ☐ 15a	b Taxable amount (see inst.)	15b	
16a	Total pensions and annuities ☐ 16a	b Taxable amount (see inst.)	16b	
17	Rental real estate, royalties, partnerships, S corporations, trusts, etc. Attach Schedule E	17	
18	Farm income or (loss). Attach Schedule F	18	
19	Unemployment compensation	19	
20a	Social security benefits . ☐ 20a	b Taxable amount (see inst.)	20b	
21	Other income. List type and amount—see instructions _Gambling_	21	
22	Add the amounts in the far right column for lines 7 through 21. This is your **total income** ►	22	

Adjusted Gross Income

If line 31 is under $28,495 (under $9,500 if a child did not live with you), see the instructions for line 54.

23a	Your IRA deduction (see instructions)	23a	
b	Spouse's IRA deduction (see instructions)	23b	
24	Moving expenses. Attach Form 3903 or 3903-F . . .	24	
25	One-half of self-employment tax. Attach Schedule SE .	25	
26	Self-employed health insurance deduction (see inst.) .	26	
27	Keogh & self-employed SEP plans. If SEP, check ► ☐	27	
28	Penalty on early withdrawal of savings	28	
29	Alimony paid. Recipient's SSN ►	29	
30	Add lines 23a through 29	30	
31	Subtract line 30 from line 22. This is your **adjusted gross income** . . . . ►	31	

For Privacy Act and Paperwork Reduction Act Notice, see page 7. | Cat. No. 11320B | Form **1040** (1996)

22

Gambling Winnings

Tax Compu-tation	32	Amount from line 31 (adjusted gross income)	32	
	33a	Check if: ☐ **You** were 65 or older, ☐ Blind; ☐ **Spouse** was 65 or older, ☐ Blind. Add the number of boxes checked above and enter the total here ► 33a		
	b	If you are married filing separately and your spouse itemizes deductions or you were a dual-status alien, see instructions and check here ► 33b ☐		
	34	Enter the larger of your: **Itemized deductions** from Schedule A, line 28, **OR** **Standard deduction** shown below for your filing status. But see the instructions if you checked any box on line 33a or b or someone can claim you as a dependent. • Single—$4,000 • Married filing jointly or Qualifying widow(er)—$6,700 • Head of household—$5,900 • Married filing separately—$3,350	34	
	35	Subtract line 34 from line 32	35	
If you want the IRS to figure your tax, see instructions for line 37.	36	If line 32 is $88,475 or less, multiply $2,550 by the total number of exemptions claimed on line 6d. If line 32 is over $88,475, see the worksheet in the inst. for the amount to enter	36	
	37	**Taxable income.** Subtract line 36 from line 35. If line 36 is more than line 35, enter -0-	37	
	38	**Tax.** See instructions. Check if total includes any tax from **a** ☐ Form(s) 8814 **b** ☐ Form 4972 ►	38	
Credits	39	Credit for child and dependent care expenses. Attach Form 2441	39	
	40	Credit for the elderly or the disabled. Attach Schedule R	40	
	41	Foreign tax credit. Attach Form 1116	41	
	42	Other. Check if from **a** ☐ Form 3800 **b** ☐ Form 8396 **c** ☐ Form 8801 **d** ☐ Form (specify)	42	
	43	Add lines 39 through 42	43	
	44	Subtract line 43 from line 38. If line 43 is more than line 38, enter -0- ►	44	
Other Taxes	45	Self-employment tax. Attach Schedule SE	45	
	46	Alternative minimum tax. Attach Form 6251	46	
	47	Social security and Medicare tax on tip income not reported to employer. Attach Form 4137	47	
	48	Tax on qualified retirement plans, including IRAs. If required, attach Form 5329	48	
	49	Advance earned income credit payments from Form(s) W-2	49	
	50	Household employment taxes. Attach Schedule H	50	
	51	Add lines 44 through 50. This is your **total tax** ►	51	
Payments Attach Forms W-2, W-2G, and 1099-R on the front.	52	Federal income tax withheld from Forms W-2 and 1099	52	
	53	1996 estimated tax payments and amount applied from 1995 return	53	
	54	**Earned income credit.** Attach Schedule EIC if you have a qualifying child. Nontaxable earned income: amount ► and type ►	54	
	55	Amount paid with Form 4868 (request for extension)	55	
	56	Excess social security and RRTA tax withheld (see inst.)	56	
	57	Other payments. Check if from **a** ☐ Form 2439 **b** ☐ Form 4136	57	
	58	Add lines 52 through 57. These are your **total payments** ►	58	
Refund Have it sent directly to your bank account! See inst. and fill in 60b, c, and d.	59	If line 58 is more than line 51, subtract line 51 from line 58. This is the amount you **OVERPAID** ►	59	
	60a	Amount of line 59 you want **REFUNDED TO YOU.** ►	60a	
	b	Routing number	c Type: ☐ Checking ☐ Savings	
	d	Account number		
	61	Amount of line 59 you want APPLIED TO YOUR 1997 ESTIMATED TAX ► 61		
Amount You Owe	62	If line 51 is more than line 58, subtract line 58 from line 51. This is the **AMOUNT YOU OWE.** For details on how to pay and use **Form 1040-V**, see instructions ►	62	
	63	Estimated tax penalty. Also include on line 62 63		

Sign Here
Keep a copy of this return for your records.

Under penalties of perjury, I declare that I have examined this return and accompanying schedules and statements, and to the best of my knowledge and belief, they are true, correct, and complete. Declaration of preparer (other than taxpayer) is based on all information of which preparer has any knowledge.

Your signature | Date | Your occupation

Spouse's signature. If a joint return, BOTH must sign. | Date | Spouse's occupation

Paid Preparer's Use Only

Preparer's signature | Date | Check if self-employed ☐ | Preparer's social security no.

Firm's name (or yours if self-employed) and address | EIN | ZIP code

23

Gambling losses are reported on Schedule A-Itemized Deductions, in the section designated "Other Itemized Deductions". The words Gambling Losses must be inserted in the space provided.

Gambling Winnings

SCHEDULES A&B (Form 1040) Department of the Treasury Internal Revenue Service (99)	Schedule A—Itemized Deductions (Schedule B is on back) ► Attach to Form 1040. ► See Instructions for Schedules A and B (Form 1040).	OMB No. 1545-0074 1996 Attachment Sequence No. 07
Name(s) shown on Form 1040		Your social security number

Medical and Dental Expenses		Caution: *Do not include expenses reimbursed or paid by others.*		
	1	Medical and dental expenses (see page A-1)	1	
	2	Enter amount from Form 1040, line 32. ⌐2 ⌐		
	3	Multiply line 2 above by 7.5% (.075)	3	
	4	Subtract line 3 from line 1. If line 3 is more than line 1, enter -0-		4
Taxes You Paid (See page A-1.)	5	State and local income taxes	5	
	6	Real estate taxes (see page A-2)	6	
	7	Personal property taxes	7	
	8	Other taxes. List type and amount ►	8	
	9	Add lines 5 through 8		9
Interest You Paid (See page A-2.)	10	Home mortgage interest and points reported to you on Form 1098	10	
	11	Home mortgage interest not reported to you on Form 1098. If paid to the person from whom you bought the home, see page A-2 and show that person's name, identifying no., and address ►	11	
Note: Personal interest is not deductible.	12	Points not reported to you on Form 1098. See page A-3 for special rules	12	
	13	Investment interest. If required, attach Form 4952. (See page A-3.)	13	
	14	Add lines 10 through 13		14
Gifts to Charity If you made a gift and got a benefit for it, see page A-3.	15	Gifts by cash or check. If you made any gift of $250 or more, see page A-3	15	
	16	Other than by cash or check. If any gift of $250 or more, see page A-3. If over $500, you **MUST** attach Form 8283	16	
	17	Carryover from prior year	17	
	18	Add lines 15 through 17		18
Casualty and Theft Losses	19	Casualty or theft loss(es). Attach Form 4684. (See page A-4.)		19
Job Expenses and Most Other Miscellaneous Deductions (See page A-4 for expenses to deduct here.)	20	Unreimbursed employee expenses—job travel, union dues, job education, etc. If required, you **MUST** attach Form 2106 or 2106-EZ. (See page A-4.) ►	20	
	21	Tax preparation fees	21	
	22	Other expenses—investment, safe deposit box, etc. List type and amount ►	22	
	23	Add lines 20 through 22	23	
	24	Enter amount from Form 1040, line 32. ⌐24 ⌐		
	25	Multiply line 24 above by 2% (.02)	25	
	26	Subtract line 25 from line 23. If line 25 is more than line 23, enter -0-		26
Other Miscellaneous Deductions	27	Other—from list on page A-4. List type and amount ► .... Gambling Losses		27
Total Itemized Deductions	28	Is Form 1040, line 32, over $117,950 (over $58,975 if married filing separately)? **NO.** Your deduction is not limited. Add the amounts in the far right column for lines 4 through 27. Also, enter on Form 1040, line 34, the **larger** of this amount or your standard deduction. **YES.** Your deduction may be limited. See page A-5 for the amount to enter.	►	28

For Paperwork Reduction Act Notice, see Form 1040 instructions.	Cat. No. 11330X	Schedule A (Form 1040) 1996

Chapter
Six

Preparing a Tax Return

Beware of This Hidden Tax Trap!!

When preparing their taxes, gamblers too often make the mistake of assuming that a given amount of winnings will be offset, or canceled out, by an equal amount of gambling losses, and that is **NOT NECESSARILY SO!** The danger lies in the fact that gambling losses, like any other itemized deduction, have no effect whatsoever on your Adjusted Gross Income, which can effect many other tax calculations, including the amount of tax on your social security benefits, the amount you can deduct for medical expenses, and so forth. (See page 9, question 10).

In the following example, you will see how this tax trap affected the return of John and Jane Taxpayer.

Facts:

John and Jane Taxpayer are both retired and are 64 years old. They have income from the following sources:

(1) Savings accounts and certificates of deposits – $2,500.

(2) Fully taxable dividends from a stock they own – $600.

(3) John is a retired corporate manager and receives a taxable pension of $20,000 per year from the company.
Jane is a retired school teacher and receives a taxable pension of $16,000.
Their combined pensions total $36,000.

(4) John and Jane's combined social security benefits are $14,500.

(5) John and Jane own their home. During 1996, they paid $1,600 in real estate taxes and $750 in mortgage interest.

(6) They also paid $150 in personal property taxes.

(7) During the year they made deductible gifts to charities in the amount of $1,200.

(8) John and Jane have a total of $5,600 withheld from their pensions for federal income taxes.
This information has been recorded and referenced on the following tax returns.

Situation 1:

While reviewing their tax return, they noticed the standard deduction amount (Form 1040, Line 34) was larger than their itemized deduction amount (Schedule A, Line 29). Therefore, they were entitled to deduct the larger standard deduction amount. They also noticed they were receiving a refund of $305 which was what they were accustomed to. John and Jane's tax return is presented on the following pages.

If a husband and wife file a joint return for a taxable year, the combined losses of the spouses from wagering transactions are allowed to the extent of their combined gains from wagering transactions.

Reg. 1.165-10

Situation 1

Form 1040	Department of the Treasury—Internal Revenue Service **U.S. Individual Income Tax Return**	**1996**	(99) IRS Use Only—Do not write or staple in this space.

For the year Jan. 1–Dec. 31, 1996, or other tax year beginning , 1996, ending , 19 | OMB No. 1545-0074

Label (See page 11.)

Your first name and initial: JOHN — Last name: TAXPAYER — Your social security number: 001 01 0001

If a joint return, spouse's first name and initial: JANE — Last name: TAXPAYER — Spouse's social security number: 002 02 0002

Use the IRS label. Otherwise, please print or type.

Home address (number and street). If you have a P.O. box, see page 11.: 123 ANY STREET — Apt. no.

City, town or post office, state, and ZIP code. If you have a foreign address, see page 11.: ANYWHERE PA 10001

For help finding line instructions, see pages 2 and 3 in the booklet.

Presidential Election Campaign (See page 11.)

	Yes	No	Note: Checking "Yes" will not change your tax or reduce your refund.
Do you want $3 to go to this fund?	X		
If a joint return, does your spouse want $3 to go to this fund?	X		

Filing Status

Check only one box.

1. Single
2. X Married filing joint return (even if only one had income)
3. Married filing separate return. Enter spouse's social security no. above and full name here. ▶
4. Head of household (with qualifying person). (See instructions.) If the qualifying person is a child but not your dependent, enter this child's name here. ▶
5. Qualifying widow(er) with dependent child (year spouse died ▶ 19). (See instructions.)

Exemptions

6a ☒ Yourself. If your parent (or someone else) can claim you as a dependent on his or her tax return, do not check box 6a .

b ☒ Spouse .

c Dependents:
- (1) First name / Last name
- (2) Dependent's social security number. If born in Dec. 1996, see inst.
- (3) Dependent's relationship to you
- (4) No. of months lived in your home in 1996

If more than six dependents, see the instructions for line 6c.

No. of boxes checked on lines 6a and 6b	2

No. of your children on line 6c who:
- lived with you
- did not live with you due to divorce or separation (see instructions)

Dependents on 6c not entered above

Add numbers entered on lines above ▶ | 2

d Total number of exemptions claimed . | 2

Income

Attach Copy B of your Forms W-2, W-2G, and 1099-R here.

If you did not get a W-2, see the instructions for line 7.

Enclose, but do not attach, any payment. Also, please enclose Form 1040-V (see the instructions for line 62).

7	Wages, salaries, tips, etc. Attach Form(s) W-2	7	
8a	Taxable interest. Attach Schedule B if over $400	8a	2,500 (1)
b	Tax-exempt interest. DO NOT include on line 8a	8b	
9	Dividend income. Attach Schedule B if over $400	9	600 (2)
10	Taxable refunds, credits, or offsets of state and local income taxes (see instructions)	10	
11	Alimony received	11	
12	Business income or (loss). Attach Schedule C or C-EZ	12	
13	Capital gain or (loss). If required, attach Schedule D	13	
14	Other gains or (losses). Attach Form 4797	14	
15a	Total IRA distributions . 15a	b Taxable amount (see inst.) 15b	
16a	Total pensions and annuities 16a	b Taxable amount (see inst.) 16b	36,000 (3)
17	Rental real estate, royalties, partnerships, S corporations, trusts. etc. Attach Schedule E	17	
18	Farm income or (loss). Attach Schedule F	18	
19	Unemployment compensation	19	
20a	Social security benefits 20a (4)14,500	b Taxable amount (see inst.) 20b	7,998
21	Other income. List type and amount—see instructions	21	
22	Add the amounts in the far right column for lines 7 through 21. This is your **total income** ▶	22	47,098

Adjusted Gross Income

If line 31 is under $28,495 (under $9,500 if a child did not live with you), see the instructions for line 54.

23a	Your IRA deduction (see instructions)	23a	
b	Spouse's IRA deduction (see instructions)	23b	
24	Moving expenses. Attach Form 3903 or 3903-F	24	
25	One-half of self-employment tax. Attach Schedule SE	25	
26	Self-employed health insurance deduction (see inst.)	26	
27	Keogh & self-employed SEP plans. If SEP, check ▶ ☐	27	
28	Penalty on early withdrawal of savings	28	
29	Alimony paid. Recipient's SSN ▶	29	
30	Add lines 23a through 29	30	
31	Subtract line 30 from line 22. This is your **adjusted gross income** ▶	31	47,098

For Privacy Act and Paperwork Reduction Act Notice, see page 7. — Cat. No. 11320B — Form **1040** (1996)

Situation 1

Form 1040 (1996)			Page **2**

Tax Compu-tation	32	Amount from line 31 (adjusted gross income)	**32**	47,098
	33a	Check if: ☐ **You** were 65 or older, ☐ Blind; ☐ **Spouse** was 65 or older, ☐ Blind. Add the number of boxes checked above and enter the total here . . . . ▶ **33a**		
	b	If you are married filing separately and your spouse itemizes deductions or you were a dual-status alien, see instructions and check here . . . . . ▶ **33b** ☐		
	34	Enter the larger of your: { Itemized deductions from Schedule A, line 28, OR Standard deduction shown below for your filing status. **But** see the instructions if you checked any box on line 33a or b **or** someone can claim you as a dependent. • Single—$4,000 • Married filing jointly or Qualifying widow(er)—$6,700 • Head of household—$5,900 • Married filing separately—$3,350 }	**34**	6,700
	35	Subtract line 34 from line 32	**35**	40,398
If you want the IRS to figure your tax, see the instructions for line 37.	36	If line 32 is $88,475 or less, multiply $2,550 by the total number of exemptions claimed on line 6d. If line 32 is over $88,475, see the worksheet in the inst. for the amount to enter .	**36**	5,100
	37	**Taxable income.** Subtract line 36 from line 35. If line 36 is more than line 35, enter -0- .	**37**	35,298
	38	**Tax.** See instructions. Check if total includes any tax from **a** ☐ Form(s) 8814 **b** ☐ Form 4972 . . . . ▶	**38**	5,295
Credits	39	Credit for child and dependent care expenses. Attach Form 2441 **39**		
	40	Credit for the elderly or the disabled. Attach Schedule R . . **40**		
	41	Foreign tax credit. Attach Form 1116 . . . . **41**		
	42	Other. Check if from **a** ☐ Form 3800 **b** ☐ Form 8396 **c** ☐ Form 8801 **d** ☐ Form (specify) _____ **42**		
	43	Add lines 39 through 42	**43**	0
	44	Subtract line 43 from line 38. If line 43 is more than line 38, enter -0-. . . . . . . ▶	**44**	5,295
Other Taxes	45	Self-employment tax. Attach Schedule SE	**45**	
	46	Alternative minimum tax. Attach Form 6251	**46**	
	47	Social security and Medicare tax on tip income not reported to employer. Attach Form 4137 . .	**47**	
	48	Tax on qualified retirement plans, including IRAs. If required, attach Form 5329	**48**	
	49	Advance earned income credit payments from Form(s) W-2	**49**	
	50	Household employment taxes. Attach Schedule H	**50**	
	51	Add lines 44 through 50. This is your **total tax** . . . . ▶	**51**	5,295
Payments	52	Federal income tax withheld from Forms W-2 and 1099 . . **52** (8) 5,600		
	53	1996 estimated tax payments and amount applied from 1995 return . **53**		
	54	**Earned income credit.** Attach Schedule EIC if you have a qualifying child. Nontaxable earned income: amount ▶ [ ] and type ▶ **54**		
Attach Forms W-2, W-2G, and 1099-R on the front.	55	Amount paid with Form 4868 (request for extension) . . . **55**		
	56	Excess social security and RRTA tax withheld (see inst.) . . **56**		
	57	Other payments. Check if from **a** ☐ Form 2439 **b** ☐ Form 4136 **57**		
	58	Add lines 52 through 57. These are your **total payments** . . . . ▶	**58**	5,600
Refund	59	If line 58 is more than line 51, subtract line 51 from line 58. This is the amount you **OVERPAID** . ▶	**59**	305
Have it sent directly to your bank account! See inst. and fill in 60b, c, and d.	60a	Amount of line 59 you want **REFUNDED TO YOU.** . . . . ▶	**60a**	305
	▶ b	Routing number [ ] **c** Type: ☐ Checking ☐ Savings		
	▶ d	Account number [ ]		
	61	Amount of line 59 you want APPLIED TO YOUR 1997 ESTIMATED TAX ▶ **61**		
Amount You Owe	62	If line 51 is more than line 58, subtract line 58 from line 51. This is the **AMOUNT YOU OWE.** For details on how to pay and use **Form 1040-V,** see instructions . . . . ▶	**62**	
	63	Estimated tax penalty. Also include on line 62 . . . . . **63**		

Sign Here	Under penalties of perjury, I declare that I have examined this return and accompanying schedules and statements, and to the best of my knowledge and belief, they are true, correct, and complete. Declaration of preparer (other than taxpayer) is based on all information of which preparer has any knowledge.		
Keep a copy of this return for your records.	Your signature ▶	Date	Your occupation Retired
	Spouse's signature. If a joint return, BOTH must sign. ▶	Date	Spouse's occupation Retired
Paid Preparer's Use Only	Preparer's signature ▶	Date	Check if self-employed ☐	Preparer's social security no.
	Firm's name (or yours if self-employed) and address ▶		EIN
			ZIP code

Situation 1

SCHEDULES A&B (Form 1040)	Schedule A—Itemized Deductions (Schedule B is on back)	OMB No. 1545-0074 **1996** Attachment Sequence No. 07

Department of the Treasury Internal Revenue Service (99) ▶ Attach to Form 1040. ▶ See Instructions for Schedules A and B (Form 1040).

Name(s) shown on Form 1040: JOHN AND JANE TAXPAYER
Your social security number: 001 : 01 : 0001

Medical and Dental Expenses
- Caution: Do not include expenses reimbursed or paid by others.
1. Medical and dental expenses (see page A-1) 1
2. Enter amount from Form 1040, line 32. | 2 |
3. Multiply line 2 above by 7.5% (.075) 3
4. Subtract line 3 from line 1. If line 3 is more than line 1, enter -0- . . . 4

Taxes You Paid (See page A-1.)
5. State and local income taxes 5
6. Real estate taxes (see page A-2) . . . . 6 (5)1,600
7. Personal property taxes 7 (6) 150
8. Other taxes. List type and amount ▶ 8
9. Add lines 5 through 8 . . . . 9 **1,750**

Interest You Paid (See page A-2.)
10. Home mortgage interest and points reported to you on Form 1098 . 10 (5) 750
11. Home mortgage interest not reported to you on Form 1098. If paid to the person from whom you bought the home, see page A-2 and show that person's name, identifying no., and address ▶ 11

Note: Personal interest is not deductible.
12. Points not reported to you on Form 1098. See page A-3 for special rules. 12
13. Investment interest. If required, attach Form 4952. (See page A-3.) . . . 13
14. Add lines 10 through 13 . . . . 14 **750**

Gifts to Charity If you made a gift and got a benefit for it, see page A-3.
15. Gifts by cash or check. If you made any gift of $250 or more, see page A-3 . . . . 15 (7)1,200
16. Other than by cash or check. If any gift of $250 or more, see page A-3. If over $500, you MUST attach Form 8283 16
17. Carryover from prior year 17
18. Add lines 15 through 17 . . . . 18 **1,200**

Casualty and Theft Losses
19. Casualty or theft loss(es). Attach Form 4684. (See page A-4.) 19

Job Expenses and Most Other Miscellaneous Deductions (See page A-4 for expenses to deduct here.)
20. Unreimbursed employee expenses—job travel, union dues, job education, etc. If required, you MUST attach Form 2106 or 2106-EZ. (See page A-4.) ▶ 20
21. Tax preparation fees 21
22. Other expenses—investment, safe deposit box, etc. List type and amount ▶ 22
23. Add lines 20 through 22 23
24. Enter amount from Form 1040, line 32. | 24 |
25. Multiply line 24 above by 2% (.02) 25
26. Subtract line 25 from line 23. If line 25 is more than line 23, enter -0- . . . 26

Other Miscellaneous Deductions
27. Other—from list on page A-4. List type and amount ▶ 27

Total Itemized Deductions
28. Is Form 1040, line 32, over $117,950 (over $58,975 if married filing separately)?
- NO. Your deduction is not limited. Add the amounts in the far right column for lines 4 through 27. Also, enter on Form 1040, line 34, the larger of this amount or your standard deduction.
- YES. Your deduction may be limited. See page A-5 for the amount to enter. ▶ 28 **3,700**

For Paperwork Reduction Act Notice, see Form 1040 instructions. Cat. No. 11330X Schedule A (Form 1040) 1996

Situation 1

	OMB No. 1545-0074 Page **2**

Name(s) shown on Form 1040. Do not enter name and social security number if shown on other side.

JOHN AND JANE TAXPAYER

Your social security number
001 : 01 :0001

Schedule B—Interest and Dividend Income

Attachment Sequence No. **08**

Part I
Interest Income

(See page B-1.)

Note: If you had over $400 in taxable interest income, you must also complete Part III.

1 List name of payer. If any interest is from a seller-financed mortgage and the buyer used the property as a personal residence, see page B-1 and list this interest first. Also, show that buyer's social security number and address ▶

	Amount
LOCAL BANK AND TRUST	850
LOCAL SAVINGS AND LOAN	1,250
LOCAL CREDIT UNION	400

Note: If you received a Form 1099-INT, Form 1099-OID, or substitute statement from a brokerage firm, list the firm's name as the payer and enter the total interest shown on that form.

2 Add the amounts on line 1	**2**	2,500
3 Excludable interest on series EE U.S. savings bonds issued after 1989 from Form 8815, line 14. You MUST attach Form 8815 to Form 1040	**3**	
4 Subtract line 3 from line 2. Enter the result here and on Form 1040, line 8a ▶	**4**	2,500	(1)

Part II
Dividend Income

(See page B-1.)

Note: If you had over $400 in gross dividends and/or other distributions on stock, you must also complete Part III.

5 List name of payer. Include gross dividends and/or other distributions on stock here. Any capital gain distributions and nontaxable distributions will be deducted on lines 7 and 8 ▶

	Amount
ANY CORPORATION	600

Note: If you received a Form 1099-DIV or substitute statement from a brokerage firm, list the firm's name as the payer and enter the total dividends shown on that form.

6 Add the amounts on line 5	**6**	600
7 Capital gain distributions. Enter here and on Schedule D* . **7**		
8 Nontaxable distributions. (See the inst. for Form 1040, line 9.) **8**		
9 Add lines 7 and 8	**9**	
10 Subtract line 9 from line 6. Enter the result here and on Form 1040, line 9 . ▶	**10**	600	(2)

*If you do not need Schedule D to report any other gains or losses, see the instructions for Form 1040, line 13.

Part III
Foreign Accounts and Trusts

(See page B-1.)

You must complete this part if you **(a)** had over $400 of interest or dividends; **(b)** had a foreign account; or **(c)** received a distribution from, or were a grantor of, or a transferor to, a foreign trust.

	Yes	No
11a At any time during 1996, did you have an interest in or a signature or other authority over a financial account in a foreign country, such as a bank account, securities account, or other financial account? See page B-1 for exceptions and filing requirements for Form TD F 90-22.1 . . .		X
b If "Yes," enter the name of the foreign country ▶		
12 During 1996, did you receive a distribution from, or were you the grantor of, or transferor to, a foreign trust? If "Yes," see page B-2 for other forms you may have to file		X

For Paperwork Reduction Act Notice, see Form 1040 instructions.

Schedule B (Form 1040) 1996

Situation 1

Social Security Benefits Worksheet—Lines 20a and 20b
(keep for your records)

If you are married filing separately and you lived apart from your spouse for all of 1995, enter "D" to the left of line 20a.

1. Enter the total amount from box 5 of all your Forms SSA-1099 and RRB-1099 . . . . 1. **14,500**
   Note: *If line 1 is zero or less, stop; none of your social security benefits are taxable. Otherwise, go to line 2.*

2. Enter one-half of line 1 . . . . 2. **7,250**

3. Add the amounts on Form 1040, lines 7, 8a, 9 through 14, 15b, 16b, 17 through 19, and 21. Do not include amounts from box 5 of Forms SSA-1099 or RRB-1099 3. **39,100**

4. Enter the amount, if any, from Form 1040, line 8b . . 4. _____

5. Add lines 2, 3, and 4 . . . . 5. **46,350**

6. Enter the amount from Form 1040, line 30 . . . . 6. _____

7. Subtract line 6 from line 5 . . . . 7. **46,350**

8. Enter $25,000 ($32,000 if married filing jointly; $0 if married filing separately and you lived with your spouse at any time in 1995) 8. **32,000**

9. Subtract line 8 from line 7. If zero or less, enter -0- . . 9. **14,350**
   Is line 9 more than zero?
   No. Stop; none of your social security benefits are taxable. Do not enter any amounts on lines 20a or 20b of Form 1040. But if you are married filing separately and you lived apart from your spouse for all of 1995, enter -0- on line 20b. Be sure to enter "D" to the left of line 20a.
   Yes. Go to line 10.

10. Enter $9,000 ($12,000 if married filing jointly; $0 if married filing separately and you lived with your spouse at any time in 1995) 10. **12,000**

11. Subtract line 10 from line 9. If zero or less, enter -0- . 11. **2,350**

12. Enter the smaller of line 9 or line 10 . . . . . . 12. **12,000**

13. Enter one-half of line 12 . . . . 13. **6,000**

14. Enter the smaller of line 2 or line 13 . . . . . . 14. **6,000**

15. Multiply line 11 by 85% (.85). If line 11 is zero, enter -0- 15. **1,998**

16. Add lines 14 and 15 . . . . 16. **7,998**

17. Multiply line 1 by 85% (.85) 17. **12,325**

18. Taxable social security benefits. Enter the smaller of line 16 or line 17 . . . . 18. **7,998**

   • Enter the amount from line 1 on Form 1040, line 20a.
   • Enter the amount from line 18 on Form 1040, line 20b.

TIP *If part of your benefits are taxable for 1995 and they include benefits paid in 1995 that were for an earlier year, you may be able to reduce the taxable amount shown on the worksheet. Get Pub. 915 for details.*

The 1996 version of this form was not available at the time of printing.

Situation 2:

Since they retired, they used their refund to offset some of their expenses on their annual trip to the casino. As they began to plan this year's trip, Jane remembered that she had won $2,500 on last year's trip. Luckily, they had not signed and mailed their return. John thought it would be no problem to change the return since they had documented gambling losses in excess of $2,500 during the year, and knew they were permitted to offset gambling winnings with losses. After reviewing the tax filing instructions, John and Jane determined the $2,500 gambling winnings had to be reported on Form 1040, Line 21. Their gambling losses, to the extent of their gambling winnings, had to be recorded on Schedule A-Itemized Deductions, Line 27.

Then they began to recalculate their gross income.

Their first surprise was that a **larger portion of their social security is taxable.** Without the $2,500 of gambling winnings, $7,998 of the $14,500 they received is taxable. After reporting their gambling winnings, the taxable portion of their social security is now $10,123, an increase of $2,125.

Their next surprise was the deduction they were entitled to on Form 1040, Line 34. Since their itemized deduction amount, including the $2,500 of gambling losses, was still below the standard deduction amount, they received **no benefit from the gambling losses.**

The final surprise was the bottom line. Instead of receiving a refund of $305, they now owed $388.

Situation 2

Form **1040**	Department of the Treasury—Internal Revenue Service **U.S. Individual Income Tax Return** 1996	(99) IRS Use Only—Do not write or staple in this space.		

For the year Jan. 1–Dec. 31, 1996, or other tax year beginning , 1996, ending , 19   OMB No. 1545-0074

Label (See page 11.)
Use the IRS label. Otherwise, please print or type.

Your first name and initial: **JOHN**   Last name: **TAXPAYER**   Your social security number: **001 01 0001**

If a joint return, spouse's first name and initial: **JANE**   Last name: **TAXPAYER**   Spouse's social security number: **002 02 0002**

Home address (number and street). If you have a P.O. box, see page 11. **123 ANY STREET**   Apt. no.

For help finding line instructions, see pages 2 and 3 in the booklet.

City, town or post office, state, and ZIP code. If you have a foreign address, see page 11. **ANYWHERE PA 10001**

Presidential Election Campaign (See page 11.)
Do you want $3 to go to this fund? ...... Yes [ ] No [X]
If a joint return, does your spouse want $3 to go to this fund? ..... Yes [ ] No [X]

Note: Checking "Yes" will not change your tax or reduce your refund.

Filing Status
Check only one box.

1 [ ] Single
2 [X] Married filing joint return (even if only one had income)
3 [ ] Married filing separate return. Enter spouse's social security no. above and full name here. ▶
4 [ ] Head of household (with qualifying person). (See instructions.) If the qualifying person is a child but not your dependent, enter this child's name here. ▶
5 [ ] Qualifying widow(er) with dependent child (year spouse died ▶ 19). (See instructions.)

Exemptions

6a [X] Yourself. If your parent (or someone else) can claim you as a dependent on his or her tax return, **do not** check box 6a .
b [X] Spouse . . . .

No. of boxes checked on lines 6a and 6b: **2**

c Dependents:
(1) First name   Last name
(2) Dependent's social security number. If born in Dec. 1996, see inst.
(3) Dependent's relationship to you
(4) No. of months lived in your home in 1996

No. of your children on line 6c who:
• lived with you
• did not live with you due to divorce or separation (see instructions)
Dependents on 6c not entered above

If more than six dependents, see the instructions for line 6c.

Add numbers entered on lines above ▶ **2**

d Total number of exemptions claimed . . . .

Income

Attach Copy B of your Forms W-2, W-2G, and 1099-R here.

If you did not get a W-2, see the instructions for line 7.

Enclose, but do not attach, any payment. Also, please enclose Form 1040-V (see the instructions for line 62).

7	Wages, salaries, tips, etc. Attach Form(s) W-2	7	
8a	Taxable interest. Attach Schedule B if over $400	8a	2,500	(1)
b	Tax-exempt interest. DO NOT include on line 8a . 8b		
9	Dividend income. Attach Schedule B if over $400	9	600	(2)
10	Taxable refunds, credits, or offsets of state and local income taxes (see instructions) .	10	
11	Alimony received	11	
12	Business income or (loss). Attach Schedule C or C-EZ	12	
13	Capital gain or (loss). If required, attach Schedule D	13	
14	Other gains or (losses). Attach Form 4797	14	
15a	Total IRA distributions . . 15a	b Taxable amount (see inst.)	15b	
16a	Total pensions and annuities 16a	b Taxable amount (see inst.)	16b	36,000	(3)
17	Rental real estate, royalties, partnerships, S corporations, trusts, etc. Attach Schedule E	17	
18	Farm income or (loss). Attach Schedule F	18	
19	Unemployment compensation	19	
20a	Social security benefits 20a (4)14,500	b Taxable amount (see inst.)	20b	10,123	
21	Other income. List type and amount—see instructions GAMBLING 2,500	21	2,500	
22	Add the amounts in the far right column for lines 7 through 21. This is your **total income** ▶	22	51,723	

Adjusted Gross Income

If line 31 is under $28,495 (under $9,500 if a child did not live with you), see the instructions for line 54.

23a	Your IRA deduction (see instructions)	23a	
b	Spouse's IRA deduction (see instructions)	23b	
24	Moving expenses. Attach Form 3903 or 3903-F . . .	24	
25	One-half of self-employment tax. Attach Schedule SE .	25	
26	Self-employed health insurance deduction (see inst.) . .	26	
27	Keogh & self-employed SEP plans. If SEP, check ▶ [ ]	27	
28	Penalty on early withdrawal of savings	28	
29	Alimony paid. Recipient's SSN ▶	29	
30	Add lines 23a through 29	30	
31	Subtract line 30 from line 22. This is your **adjusted gross income** . . . . ▶	31	51,723	

For Privacy Act and Paperwork Reduction Act Notice, see page 7.   Cat. No. 11320B   Form **1040** (1996)

Situation 2

Form 1040 (1996)						Page **2**
Tax Computation	32	Amount from line 31 (adjusted gross income)			32	51,723
	33a	Check if: ☐ **You** were 65 or older, ☐ Blind; ☐ **Spouse** was 65 or older, ☐ Blind. Add the number of boxes checked above and enter the total here ▶ 33a				
	b	If you are married filing separately and your spouse itemizes deductions or you were a dual-status alien, see instructions and check here ▶ 33b ☐				
	34	Enter the larger of your: **Itemized deductions** from Schedule A, line 28, **OR** **Standard deduction** shown below for your filing status. **But see the** instructions if you checked any box on line 33a or b or someone can claim you as a dependent. • Single—$4,000 • Married filing jointly or Qualifying widow(er)—$6,700 • Head of household—$5,900 • Married filing separately—$3,350			34	6,700
	35	Subtract line 34 from line 32			35	45,023
If you want the IRS to figure your tax, see the instructions for line 37.	36	If line 32 is $88,475 or less, multiply $2,550 by the total number of exemptions claimed on line 6d. If line 32 is over $88,475, see the worksheet in the inst. for the amount to enter			36	5,100
	37	**Taxable income.** Subtract line 36 from line 35. If line 36 is more than line 35, enter -0-			37	39,923
	38	**Tax.** See instructions. Check if total includes any tax from a ☐ Form(s) 8814 b ☐ Form 4972 ▶			38	5,988
Credits	39	Credit for child and dependent care expenses. Attach Form 2441	39			
	40	Credit for the elderly or the disabled. Attach Schedule R	40			
	41	Foreign tax credit. Attach Form 1116	41			
	42	Other. Check if from a ☐ Form 3800 b ☐ Form 8396 c ☐ Form 8801 d ☐ Form (specify)	42			
	43	Add lines 39 through 42			43	0
	44	Subtract line 43 from line 38. If line 43 is more than line 38, enter -0- ▶			44	5,988
Other Taxes	45	Self-employment tax. Attach Schedule SE			45	
	46	Alternative minimum tax. Attach Form 6251			46	
	47	Social security and Medicare tax on tip income not reported to employer. Attach Form 4137			47	
	48	Tax on qualified retirement plans, including IRAs. If required, attach Form 5329			48	
	49	Advance earned income credit payments from Form(s) W-2			49	
	50	Household employment taxes. Attach Schedule H			50	
	51	Add lines 44 through 50. This is your **total tax** ▶			51	5,988
Payments	52	Federal income tax withheld from Forms W-2 and 1099	52	(8) 5,600		
	53	1996 estimated tax payments and amount applied from 1995 return	53			
	54	**Earned income credit.** Attach Schedule EIC if you have a qualifying child. Nontaxable earned income: amount ▶ and type ▶	54			
Attach Forms W-2, W-2G, and 1099-R on the front.	55	Amount paid with Form 4868 (request for extension)	55			
	56	Excess social security and RRTA tax withheld (see inst.)	56			
	57	Other payments. Check if from a ☐ Form 2439 b ☐ Form 4136	57			
	58	Add lines 52 through 57. These are your **total payments** ▶			58	5,600
Refund	59	If line 58 is more than line 51, subtract line 51 from line 58. This is the amount you **OVERPAID** ▶			59	
Have it sent directly to your bank account! See inst. and fill in 60b, c, and d.	60a	Amount of line 59 you want **REFUNDED TO YOU.** ▶			60a	
	b	Routing number ▢▢▢▢▢▢▢▢▢ c Type: ☐ Checking ☐ Savings				
	d	Account number ▢▢▢▢▢▢▢▢▢▢▢▢▢▢▢▢▢				
	61	Amount of line 59 you want APPLIED TO YOUR 1997 ESTIMATED TAX ▶	61			
Amount You Owe	62	If line 51 is more than line 58, subtract line 58 from line 51. This is the **AMOUNT YOU OWE.** For details on how to pay and use **Form 1040-V,** see instructions ▶			62	388
	63	Estimated tax penalty. Also include on line 62	63			
Sign Here Keep a copy of this return for your records.		Under penalties of perjury, I declare that I have examined this return and accompanying schedules and statements, and to the best of my knowledge and belief, they are true, correct, and complete. Declaration of preparer (other than taxpayer) is based on all information of which preparer has any knowledge.				
		Your signature ▶	Date	Your occupation RETIRED		
		Spouse's signature. if a joint return BOTH must sign. ▶	Date	Spouse's occupation RETIRED		
Paid Preparer's Use Only		Preparer's signature ▶	Date	Check if self-employed ☐	Preparer's social security no.	
		Firm's name (or yours if self-employed) and address ▶		EIN ZIP code		

Situation 2

SCHEDULES A&B
(Form 1040)

Department of the Treasury
Internal Revenue Service (99)

Schedule A—Itemized Deductions
(Schedule B is on back)

▶ Attach to Form 1040. ▶ See Instructions for Schedules A and B (Form 1040).

OMB No. 1545-0074

1996

Attachment
Sequence No. **07**

Name(s) shown on Form 1040

JOHN AND JANE TAXPAYER

Your social security number

001 : 01 : 0001

Medical and Dental Expenses		Caution: Do not include expenses reimbursed or paid by others.		
	1	Medical and dental expenses (see page A-1)	1	
	2	Enter amount from Form 1040, line 32. ⌞2⌟		
	3	Multiply line 2 above by 7.5% (.075)	3	
	4	Subtract line 3 from line 1. If line 3 is more than line 1, enter -0-	**4**	
Taxes You Paid (See page A-1.)	5	State and local income taxes	5	
	6	Real estate taxes (see page A-2)	6 (5)1,600	
	7	Personal property taxes	7 (6) 150	
	8	Other taxes. List type and amount ▶	8	
	9	Add lines 5 through 8	**9**	1,750
Interest You Paid (See page A-2.)	10	Home mortgage interest and points reported to you on Form 1098	10 (5) 750	
	11	Home mortgage interest not reported to you on Form 1098. If paid to the person from whom you bought the home, see page A-2 and show that person's name, identifying no., and address ▶	11	
Note: Personal interest is not deductible.	12	Points not reported to you on Form 1098. See page A-3 for special rules	12	
	13	Investment interest. If required, attach Form 4952. (See page A-3.)	13	
	14	Add lines 10 through 13	**14**	750
Gifts to Charity If you made a gift and got a benefit for it, see page A-3.	15	Gifts by cash or check. If you made any gift of $250 or more, see page A-3	15 (7)1,200	
	16	Other than by cash or check. If any gift of $250 or more, see page A-3. If over $500, you **MUST** attach Form 8283	16	
	17	Carryover from prior year	17	
	18	Add lines 15 through 17	**18**	1,200
Casualty and Theft Losses	19	Casualty or theft loss(es). Attach Form 4684. (See page A-4.)	**19**	
Job Expenses and Most Other Miscellaneous Deductions (See page A-4 for expenses to deduct here.)	20	Unreimbursed employee expenses—job travel, union dues, job education, etc. If required, you **MUST** attach Form 2106 or 2106-EZ. (See page A-4.) ▶	20	
	21	Tax preparation fees	21	
	22	Other expenses—investment, safe deposit box, etc. List type and amount ▶	22	
	23	Add lines 20 through 22	23	
	24	Enter amount from Form 1040, line 32. ⌞24⌟		
	25	Multiply line 24 above by 2% (.02)	25	
	26	Subtract line 25 from line 23. If line 25 is more than line 23, enter -0-	**26**	
Other Miscellaneous Deductions	27	Other—from list on page A-4. List type and amount ▶ . . . . GAMBLING LOSSES 2,500		
			27	2,500
Total Itemized Deductions	28	Is Form 1040, line 32, over $117,950 (over $58,975 if married filing separately)? **NO.** Your deduction is not limited. Add the amounts in the far right column for lines 4 through 27. Also, enter on Form 1040, line 34, the **larger** of this amount or your standard deduction. **YES.** Your deduction may be limited. See page A-5 for the amount to enter.	▶ 28	6,200

For Paperwork Reduction Act Notice, see Form 1040 instructions.   Cat. No. 11330X   Schedule A (Form 1040) 1996

Situation 2

Schedules A&B (Form 1040) 1996   OMB No. 1545-0074   Page **2**

Name(s) shown on Form 1040. Do not enter name and social security number if shown on other side.

JOHN AND JANE TAXPAYER

Your social security number: 001 01 0001

Attachment Sequence No. **08**

Schedule B—Interest and Dividend Income

Part I Interest Income

(See page B-1.)

Note: *If you had over $400 in taxable interest income, you must also complete Part III.*

1 List name of payer. If any interest is from a seller-financed mortgage and the buyer used the property as a personal residence, see page B-1 and list this interest first. Also, show that buyer's social security number and address ▶

Payer	Amount
LOCAL BANK AND TRUST	850
LOCAL SAVINGS AND LOAN	1,250
LOCAL CREDIT UNION	400

Note: If you received a Form 1099-INT, Form 1099-OID, or substitute statement from a brokerage firm, list the firm's name as the payer and enter the total interest shown on that form.

2 Add the amounts on line 1 .... **2** | 2,500

3 Excludable interest on series EE U.S. savings bonds issued after 1989 from Form 8815, line 14. You MUST attach Form 8815 to Form 1040 .... **3**

4 Subtract line 3 from line 2. Enter the result here and on Form 1040, line 8a ▶ **4** | 2,500 **(1)**

Part II Dividend Income

(See page B-1.)

Note: *If you had over $400 in gross dividends and/or other distributions on stock, you must also complete Part III.*

5 List name of payer. Include gross dividends and/or other distributions on stock here. Any capital gain distributions and nontaxable distributions will be deducted on lines 7 and 8 ▶

Payer	Amount
ANY CORPORATION	600

Note: If you received a Form 1099-DIV or substitute statement from a brokerage firm, list the firm's name as the payer and enter the total dividends shown on that form.

6 Add the amounts on line 5 .... **6** | 600

7 Capital gain distributions. Enter here and on Schedule D*. **7**

8 Nontaxable distributions. (See the inst. for Form 1040, line 9.) **8**

9 Add lines 7 and 8 .... **9**

10 Subtract line 9 from line 6. Enter the result here and on Form 1040, line 9 . ▶ **10** | 600 **(2)**

*If you do not need Schedule D to report any other gains or losses, see the instructions for Form 1040, line 13.

Part III Foreign Accounts and Trusts

(See page B-1.)

You must complete this part if you **(a)** had over $400 of interest or dividends; **(b)** had a foreign account; or **(c)** received a distribution from, or were a grantor of, or a transferor to, a foreign trust.

	Yes	No
11a At any time during 1996, did you have an interest in or a signature or other authority over a financial account in a foreign country, such as a bank account, securities account, or other financial account? See page B-1 for exceptions and filing requirements for Form TD F 90-22.1		X
b If "Yes," enter the name of the foreign country ▶		
12 During 1996, did you receive a distribution from, or were you the grantor of, or transferor to, a foreign trust? If "Yes," see page B-2 for other forms you may have to file		X

For Paperwork Reduction Act Notice, see Form 1040 instructions.   Schedule B (Form 1040) 1996

Situation 2

Social Security Benefits Worksheet—Lines 20a and 20b
(keep for your records)

If you are married filing separately and you **lived apart** from your spouse for all of 1995, enter "D" to the left of line 20a.

1. Enter the total amount from **box 5** of all your **Forms SSA-1099** and **RRB-1099** . . . . **1.** __14,500__

   Note: If line 1 is zero or less, stop; none of your social security benefits are taxable. Otherwise, go to line 2.

2. Enter one-half of line 1 . . . . **2.** __7,250__

3. Add the amounts on Form 1040, lines 7, 8a, 9 through 14, 15b, 16b, 17 through 19, and 21. Do not include amounts from box 5 of Forms SSA-1099 or RRB-1099 **3.** __41,600__

4. Enter the amount, if any, from Form 1040, line 8b . . **4.** _____

5. Add lines 2, 3, and 4 . . . . **5.** __48,850__

6. Enter the amount from Form 1040, line 30 . . . . . **6.** _____

7. Subtract line 6 from line 5 . . . . **7.** __48,850__

8. Enter $25,000 ($32,000 if married filing jointly; $0 if married filing separately and you lived with your spouse at any time in 1995) . . . . **8.** __32,000__

9. Subtract line 8 from line 7. If zero or less, enter -0- . . **9.** __16,850__

   Is line 9 more than zero?

   No. Stop; none of your social security benefits are taxable. Do not enter any amounts on lines 20a or 20b of Form 1040. But if you are married filing separately and you **lived apart** from your spouse for all of 1995, enter -0- on line 20b. Be sure to enter "D" to the left of line 20a.

   Yes. Go to line 10.

10. Enter $9,000 ($12,000 if married filing jointly; $0 if married filing separately and you lived with your spouse at any time in 1995) . . . . **10.** __12,000__

11. Subtract line 10 from line 9. If zero or less, enter -0- . **11.** __4,850__

12. Enter the smaller of line 9 or line 10 . . . . **12.** __12,000__

13. Enter one-half of line 12 . . . . **13.** __6,000__

14. Enter the smaller of line 2 or line 13 . . . . **14.** __6,000__

15. Multiply line 11 by 85% (.85). If line 11 is zero, enter -0- **15.** __4,123__

16. Add lines 14 and 15 . . . . **16.** __10,123__

17. Multiply line 1 by 85% (.85) . . . . **17.** __12,325__

18. **Taxable social security benefits.** Enter the smaller of line 16 or line 17 . . . . **18.** __10,123__

   • Enter the amount from line 1 on Form 1040, line 20a.

   • Enter the amount from line 18 on Form 1040, line 20b.

   TIP *If part of your benefits are taxable for 1995 **and** they include benefits paid in 1995 that were for an earlier year, you may be able to reduce the taxable amount shown on the worksheet. Get Pub. 915 for details.*

The 1996 version of this form was not available at the time of printing.

Summary:

In the case of John and Jane Taxpayer, adding $2,500 of gambling winnings to their total income had the following effect:

- It increased the taxable portion of their social security by $2,125.

- It did not increase their standard/itemized deduction amount since their itemized deductions, including the gambling losses, did not exceed the standard deduction they were entitled to.

- Even though their winnings equalled their loss, they still increased their total tax liability from $5,295 to $5,988.

Naturally the results will be different for each taxpayer. If you have gambling winnings during the year, you should review your tax situation carefully. You may even want to consider making estimated quarterly payments, to avoid problems at the end of the year.

Above all, don't assume that gambling losses will automatically offset gains, or that they won't affect your tax liability.

Gambling winnings from legal and illegal activities must be included in gross income.

Carmack v. Commissioner

Chapter
Seven

FILING AN AMENDED TAX RETURN

Had John and Jane Taxpayer filed their return and then discovered that they had omitted their gambling winnings and losses, they would have been required to file an amended tax return Form 1040X.

Form 1040X is required only after the original return has been filed. Generally, Form 1040X must be filed within three years after the date the original return was filed, and should be mailed to the Internal Revenue Service Center where the original return was sent.

A separate Form 1040X is required for each year being amended. When an amended federal return is needed, an amended state return may also be required.

Had they neglected to report their gambling activity, John and Jane Taxpayer would have filed form 1040X, which appears on the next 2 pages.

Form **1040X**			
(Rev. October 1996)	Department of the Treasury - Internal Revenue Service		OMB No. 1545-0091

Amended U.S. Individual Income Tax Return

This return is for calendar year ▶ 19 96 , OR fiscal year ended ▶ _____, 19____.

Your first name and initial JOHN	Last name TAXPAYER	Your social security number 001 01 0001
If a joint return, spouse's first name and initial JANE	Last name TAXPAYER	Spouse's social security number 002 02 0002
Home address (number and street). If you have a P.O. box, see instructions. 123 ANY STREET	Apt. no.	Telephone number (optional)
City, town or post office, state, and ZIP code. If you have a foreign address, see instructions. ANYWHERE PA 10001		For Paperwork Reduction Act Notice, see page 1 of separate instructions.

A If the name or address shown above is different from that shown on the original return, check here .... ▶ ☐

B Has original return been changed or audited by the IRS or have you been notified that it will be? .... ☐ Yes ☒ No
If notified that it will be, identify the IRS office ▶

C If you are amending your return to include any item (loss, credit, deduction, other tax benefit, or income) relating to a tax shelter required to be registered, attach Form 8271 Investor Reporting of Tax Shelter Registration Number, and
check here .... ▶ ☐

D Filing status claimed. Note: You cannot change from joint to separate returns after the due date has passed.
On original return ▶ ☐ Single ☒ Married filing joint return ☐ Married filing separate return ☐ Head of household ☐ Qualifying widow(er)
On this return ▶ ☐ Single ☒ Married filing joint return ☐ Married filing separate return ☐ Head of household ☐ Qualifying widow(er)

Income and Deductions (see instructions)
USE PART II ON PAGE 2 TO EXPLAIN ANY CHANGES

			A. As originally reported or as previously adjusted	B. Net change - Increase or (Decrease) - explain on page 2	C. Correct amount
1	Adjusted gross income (see instructions)	1	47,098	4,625	51,723
2	Itemized deductions or standard deduction	2	6,700		6,700
3	Subtract line 2 from line 1	3	40,398	4,625	45,023
4	Exemptions. If changing, fill in Parts I and II on page 2	4	5,100		5,100
5	Taxable income. Subtract line 4 from line 3	5	35,298	4,625	39,923
6	Tax (see instructions). Method used in col. C TAX RATES	6	5,295	693	5,988
7	Credits (see instructions)	7			
8	Subtract line 7 from line 6. Enter the result but not less than zero	8	5,295	693	5,988
9	Other taxes (see instructions)	9			
10	Total tax. Add lines 8 and 9	10	5,295	693	5,988
11	Federal income tax withheld and excess social security, Medicare, and RRTA taxes withheld. If changing, see instructions	11	5,600		5,600
12	Estimated tax payments	12			
13	Earned income credit	13			
14	Credits for Federal tax paid on fuels, regulated investment company, etc	14			
15	Amount paid with Form 4868, Form 2688, or Form 2350 (application for extension of time to file)		15		
16	Amount of tax paid with original return plus additional tax paid after it was filed		16		
17	Total payments. Add lines 11 through 16 in column C		17		5,600

Refund or Amount You Owe

18	Overpayment, if any, as shown on original return or as previously adjusted by the IRS		18	305
19	Subtract line 18 from line 17		19	5,295
20	AMOUNT YOU OWE. If line 10, column C, is more than line 19, enter the difference and see instructions		20	693
21	If line 10, column C, is less than line 19, enter the difference		21	
22	Amount of line 21 you want REFUNDED TO YOU		22	
23	Amount of line 21 you want APPLIED TO YOUR 19 ESTIMATED TAX	23		

Sign Here
Keep a copy of this return for your records.

Under penalties of perjury, I declare that I have filed an original return and that I have examined this amended return, including accompanying schedules and statements, and to the best of my knowledge and belief, this amended return is true, correct, and complete. Declaration of preparer (other than taxpayer) is based on all information of which the preparer has any knowledge.

▶ Your signature _____ Date _____ ▶ Spouse's signature. If a joint return, BOTH must sign. Date _____

Paid Preparer's Use Only

Preparer's signature ▶	Date	Check if self-employed ☐	Preparer's soc. sec. no.
Firm's name (or yours if self-employed) and address ▶		EIN	
		ZIP code	

0701
-06-96

LHA

Form **1040X** (Rev. 10-96)

Form 1040X (Rev. 10-95)   JOHN AND JANE TAXPAYER   001–01–0001   Page 2

Part I — Exemptions

If you are not changing your exemptions, do not complete this part.
If claiming more exemptions, complete lines 24-30 and, if applicable, line 31.
If claiming fewer exemptions, complete lines 24-29.

		A. Number originally reported	B. Net change	C. Correct number
24	Yourself and spouse **24**			
	Caution: If your parents (or someone else) can claim you as a dependent (even if they chose not to), you cannot claim an exemption for yourself.			
25	Your dependent children who lived with you **25**			
26	Your dependent children who did not live with you due to divorce or separation **26**			
27	Other dependents **27**			
28	Total number of exemptions. Add lines 24 through 27 .... **28**			
29	Multiply the number of exemptions claimed on line 28 by the amount listed below for the tax year you are amending. Enter the result here and on line 4. **29**			

Tax Year	Exemption Amount	But see the Instructions if the amount on line 1 is over:
1995	$2,500	$86,025
1994	2,450	83,850
1993	2,350	81,350
1992	2,300	78,950

30 Dependents (children and other) not claimed on original return:

Note: *If amending your 1995 return, do not complete column (b) below.*

(a) First Name	Last name	(b) Check if under age 1	(c) If age 1 or older (or born before 11/1/95 if a 1995 return), enter dependent's social security number	(d) Dependent's relationship to you	(e) No. of months lived in your home

No. of your children on line 30 who lived with you .... ▶ ☐

No. of your children on line 30 who didn't live with you due to divorce or separation .... ▶ ☐

No. of dependents on line 30 not entered above .... ▶ ☐

31 If your child listed on line 30 didn't live with you but is claimed as your dependent under a pre-1985 agreement, check here .... ▶ ☐

Part II — Explanation of Changes to Income, Deductions, and Credits

Enter the line number from page 1 for each item you are changing and give the reason for each change. Attach all supporting forms and schedules for items changed. If you don't, your Form 1040X may be returned. Be sure to include your name and social security number on any attachments.

If the change relates to a net operating loss carryback or a general business credit carryback, attach the schedule or form that shows the year in which the loss or credit occurred. See instructions. Also, check here .... ▶ ☐

LINE 1 – INCREASED TO INCLUDE GAMBLING WINNINGS   2,500
         INCREASED TO INCLUDE ADDITIONAL TAXABLE
         SOCIAL SECURITY   2,125
         TOTAL LINE 1 – COLUMN B   4,625

Part III — Presidential Election Campaign Fund

Checking below will not increase your tax or reduce your refund.

If you did not previously want to have $3 go to the fund but now want to, check here .... ▶ ☐

If a joint return and your spouse did not previously want to have $3 go to the fund but now wants to, check here .... ▶ ☐

0702
-28-96

Cohan Rule

The general rule requires the taxpayer to substantiate its deductions. Under certain circumstances a court may waive this requirement. When a taxpayer is unquestionably entitled to some deduction, but the amount is not properly substantiated the court may make an allowance based on an estimate (G. M. Cohan).
To allow the use of estimates under the Cohan Rule the court must be convinced that:

- *the expense was incurred by the taxpayer.*

- *there is a basis upon which to estimate the allowance.*

In the case of Doffin v. Commissioner, the Tax Court applied the Cohan Rule and allowed estimated losses of approximately $64,000 after the IRS allowed only $247.

The Court also estimated the taxpayer's losses under the Cohan Rule in the case of F.M. Delgozzo.

The Court determined the Cohen Rule did not apply in the case of A. Plisco since reliable figures were not available to calculate the estimates.

Author's Comment: The Cohen Rule is not an alternative to proper recordkeeping. The only way to be certain the losses you claim will be accepted is through proper documentation.

Chapter
Eight

CONCLUSION

Tax situations are very unique for gaming enthusiasts, and gambling activity requires constant monitoring and documenting. Proper planning is needed on a continuing basis to avoid unwanted tax surprises. Unfortunately, there's no way to avoid the possibility of having your tax return selected for an IRS review. But at least there is comfort and security in knowing that all necessary reporting requirements have been met. As always, consult your accountant or tax advisor with any questions you may have.

APPENDIX

Throughout the guide, substantiation requirements have been stressed. The section dealing with "Substantiating Losses" indicates the IRS has not issued a preprinted format for documenting your activity that will, without question, be accepted. Please review Chapter Three of the guide and Revenue Procedure 77-29 before you begin to keep "log" or "diary".

Losses sustained during a taxable year on wagering transactions are allowed as a deduction but only to the extent of gains during the same taxable year from wagering transactions.

Reg. 1.165-10

REFERENCES AND RESOURCES

The Internal Revenue Code of 1986

The 1995, Form 1040 Tax Package
Forms and Instructions
Department of the Treasury
Internal Revenue Service
P.O. Box 8905
Bloomington, IL 61702

Publication 525
Taxable and Nontaxable Income
Department of the Treasury
Internal Revenue Service
Cat. No. 15047D

Publication 529
Miscellaneous Deductions
Department of the Treasury
Internal Revenue Service
Cat. No. 15056O

CCH Standard Federal Tax Reported
by CCH Tax Law Editors
Commerce Clearing House, Inc.
4025 West Peterson Avenue
Chicago, IL 60646

REFERENCES AND RESOURCES
(CONTINUED)

J.K. Lasser's Your Income Tax 1995
Professional Edition
Prepared by J.K. Lasser Institute
Fifty-eighth Edition
Macmillan General Reference
A Prentice Hall Macmillan Company
15 Columbus Circle
New York, NY 10023

Wall Street Journal
200 Liberty Street
New York, NY 10281

Harrah's Survey of Casino Entertainment 1995 & 1996
Harrah's Marketing Communications
1023 Cherry Road
Memphis, TN 38117

RIA's Analysis of Federal Taxes
Copyright 1995 by Research Institute of America
90 Fifth Avenue
New York, NY 10011

Las Vegas Convention & Visitors Authority
3150 Paradise Road
Las Vegas, NV 89109
(702) 892-0711

INDEX